D0847809

AN EDWARDIAN Guide to LIFE

AN EDWARDIAN GUIDE TO LIFE

Copyright © Summersdale Publishers Ltd, 2011

With thanks to Abi McMahon

Summersdale Publishers Ltd
46 West Street
Chichester
West Sussex
PO19 1RP
UK

www.summersdale.com

Printed and bound in the Czech Republic

ISBN: 978-1-84953-193-1

AN EDWARDIAN Guide to LIFE

CORNELIA DOBBS

summersdale

CONTENTS

INTRODUCTION

An unaffected grace and charm of manner defines the well-bred classes of this golden age, skilled in the art of social intercourse and well-versed in the duties of good housekeeping. I have compiled this volume in order that those among us who strive for this may herein discover all minutiae of etiquette necessary. No circumstance – from hosting a garden party to dealing with gossip – is overlooked.

Never again will you, dear reader, fear the embarrassment that succeeds an erroneous choice of hat or glove, or the shame of curtseying on the wrong foot when you debut in front of our beloved monarchs, King Edward and Queen Alexandra. It is my sincerest hope that all who follow this wisdom shall leave behind all traces of unrefined awkwardness and coarse behaviour, and emerge a more gallant, gentle and cordial member of our society, with an exemplary household.

Cornelia Dobbs, 1908

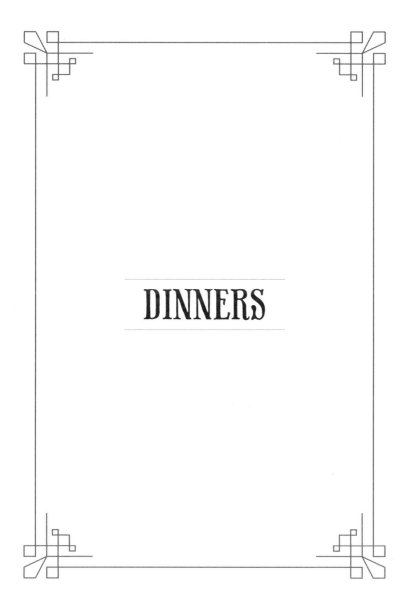

DINNERS

Table Manners

When waiting for service, do not beat the 'devil's tattoo' by drumming with your fingers on the table top; it cannot fail to irritate everyone and is the index of a vacant mind.

There is no worthier accomplishment for a man with a moustache than to take soup in an inoffensive manner. Undue noise and exaggerated action should be eliminated, and by no means should the moustache be used as an implement with which to strain the soup.

Never speak with your mouth full. Making a noise when chewing, or breathing hard when eating, are both unseemly habits, and ought to be eschewed.

It is considered vulgar to partake of the fish or soup course twice. The reason for not helping oneself twice at a dinner party is because by so doing you keep three parts of the company staring at you whilst waiting for the second course, which is spoiling, much to the annoyance of the mistress of the house.

Many people make a disgusting noise with their lips, by inhaling their breath strongly whilst taking soup – a habit which should be carefully avoided.

Try not to pick your teeth at the dinner table. However satisfactory to practice it yourself, to witness it is not pleasant.

At dinner, where common household bread is used, it should never be cut less than an inch and a half thick. There is nothing more plebeian than *thin* bread at dinner.

Eat peas with a dessert spoon; and curry also. Curry is the only meat dish that may be eaten with a spoon.

You should never ask any person at table to help you to anything; always apply to servants.

It may never cross the minds of some people to thank a servant; others say it out of graciousness of mind and manner. Offering an occasional 'thanks' to the parlourmaid or manservant would not go amiss but it must be said in a manner that will not encourage familiarity.

Table Talk

It is often the case that a number of people who meet with each other will discuss the affairs of someone who is absent. This is not only uncharitable but positively unjust. As a rule, people who unite with you in discussing the affairs of others will proceed to scandalise you the moment you depart.

Consequently, give your own opinion of people if you choose, but you are not at liberty to repeat that of others. Only fancy the result of one lady saying to another, 'Well, Emma, what do you think Miss Appleby says of you? She says that you have the thickest ankles, and the thinnest arms, of any girl in the country; with a figure like an alligator and a head like a bison!'

Be cautious also how you take the lead in conversation, unless it be forced upon you, lest people reiterate the remark cast on a certain occasion upon that *'Brummagem'* Johnson, Doctor Parr – that he was like 'a "great toe" in society; the most ignoble part of the body, yet ever thrust foremost.'

Beware: some men have a mania for Greek and Latin quotations; this is peculiarly to be avoided. It is like pulling up the stones from a tomb wherewith to kill the living. Nothing is more wearisome than pedantry.

At the table, adopt a 'patrician' tone of voice, rather than a loud and booming one.

When telling jokes, be sure to laugh afterwards.

On the subject of laughter, there is no greater ornament to conversation than the ripple of silvery notes that form the perfect laugh. Laughter is a good test of breeding – the coarse 'Haw, haw' of the uneducated tells as much. Star of light opera, Florence St John once told a newspaper how she learnt to laugh. It was English libretto H. B. Farnie that took her in hand for the laughing scene in *Madame Favart*. The actress rehearsed a descending octave staccato with the syllables 'Ha, ha' and perfected the prettiest laugh, which she admitted was worth taking some pains to achieve.

As to the grins, very few of them can be described as pleasing. Pretty teeth may redeem some of them from absolute ignominy, but, as a rule, the exhibition of whole meadows of pale pink gum is inconsonant with one's ideas of beauty.

Hosting

The hostess must shake hands with all her guests. The sole exception is that of royalty, and in this case the hostess waits for her guest to hold out his or her hand.

When the members of the party have all assembled in the drawing room, the mistress of the house will point out which lady one is to take into the dining-room, according to some real or fancied standard of precedence, rank (if there be rank), age or general importance; that is, the married before the single, &c., &c., or they will show their tact by making companions of those who are most likely to be agreeable to each other.

The King and Queen's travels to the exotic have filtered down to the humble tablecloth. Gone are the days when plain white damask was the only resource of the Edwardian housewife; brocade and ripples of pale pink-, mauve- and yellow-printed Indian silk loosely disposed in waves down the dining table is quite the thing. The colours of the moment are mauve and heliotrope. Flowers in a basket hanging from the ring where the now almost obsolete gas chandelier previously hung are among the prettiest displays I've seen.

Servants should wait at the table in clean white gloves: there are few things more disagreeable than the thumb of a clumsy waiter in your plate.

The lady of the house must appear gracious at all times. If the entire party is waiting upon one guest she must try to divert her companions with pleasant and agreeable conversation.

We shudder to think of the fatigue suffered by the hostess of past times, whose energy was so consumed by the minutiae of dinner-giving we wonder that she had breath enough to speak a word to her guests. A successful hostess knows now to leave the bulk of the work to the caterers and concentrate on the details that add the character which so contributes to the joy of the meal.

At every respectable table you will find silver forks; being broader, they are in all respects more convenient than steel for fish and vegetables.

Dressing the table for a dinner party: The table should be dressed daintily in spotless snowy linen, the glassware must gleam and the silver must be shiny and blemish-free. The table must always afford a little spare room – better to invite one friend less in number than to destroy the comfort of the entire party.

At some of the best houses, coffee is brought into the dining-room before the gentlemen quit the table – a very good custom, as it gently prevents excess. Coffee should be brought in at an hour previously appointed, without the bell being rung for it, but a sufficient interval must be allowed, lest the host seem chary of his wine. For instance, nine o'clock is a good hour, if the dinner were at six; or ten o'clock for one which commenced at seven.

ETHICS OF DRESS

Fashion and Deportment

A more ridiculous fashion cannot be conceived than that of the 'Alexandra limp'. Some foolish souls imagine it to be admiring and are of the opinion that in aping the Queen they are offering Her Majesty a compliment. We wonder at any person who would enjoy being so artlessly reminded of an unhappy illness – rheumatic fever, no less – and especially one that bore so unfortunate a consequence. Still more alarming is the notion of some ladies to alter their shoes so that one heel might be greater in height than the other. Such behaviour may be befitting a lady of fashion but never one of taste.

It is not practical for a lady to include a hat over-trimmed in her bicycling costume, no matter how much the fashion it may be. She will spend the time that should be allocated to carefully navigating her course on managing her hat, and is likely to bring herself into peril.

A gentleman will always wear an evening suit at a formal dinner party, the articles of which are dress-coat, black trousers, white or black waistcoat, and white tie. If he should dine with friends with whom he is intimate he may substitute a black tie for white, and the dinner-jacket will take the place of the coat.

Brown boots may be worn at Ascot, but certainly never in town.

A well-bred man always wears yellow kids in dancing. (So says our Parisian authority: we take exception, however, to the yellow – a tint is preferable to a decided colour.)

It is a delicate subject to hint at the incongruities of a lady's dress – yet, alas, it forces itself upon our notice when we see a lady of autumn years assume the wardrobe of spring, or a lady upon her first appearance affect singularity of dress. In a married woman a richer style of ornament is admissible. Costly elegance for her; a style of modest simplicity for the younger girl.

It may appear a simple suggestion, but experience only will show how much time might be redeemed by habits of regularity; such as putting out the shawls or whatever is intended to be worn, in readiness, instead of having to search one drawer then another.

The line of the neck is cut high, favouring the habits of our Queen and frustrating that particular party of people who are never happier than when they may cast an unhappy glance at a lady's gown and regret very much the moral deficit of youth. When a gown is worn décolletage, fashion allows for a high necklace to cover the neck.

Hair and Make-up

In abundance of hair Anglo-Saxon men often show poorly in comparison to their Latin cousins. It is no secret that men possess every inch the vanity that women do, when they feel a thing is worth being vain over, and to comment on the loss of a gentleman's hair is often to give the cut direct.

The man of declining hair must no longer fear removing his hat with the invention of Mr Edward's Harlene Hair Drill, sanctioned by the King himself. The tonic takes but a moment to apply and has caused many a man to marvel at the almost immediate abundance of hair leaping up from the head as weeds from a garden.

To the lady at the Theatre who chooses to adorn her hair with great plumes, we say some consideration to the souls behind her who also have a desire to enjoy the entertainment would not be misplaced.

The woman who uses a permanent wave machine is the victim of much hypocrisy from her husband. He is free with his scorn of the elaborate and irrational lengths a woman will go to follow fashion, but would shirk escorting us to our favoured restaurants and pet theatres should we be singular, or drab to you and me, in appearance.

Women not gifted by nature with luxuriant tresses have a good deal to celebrate in the fashion of the *transformation*. How they have watched in fear as hair has climbed ever higher while still affecting to be all the wearer's own. And how their fears must have been allayed with the introduction of the pompadour frame, over which they have but to smooth their hair to emulate the fashion.

The arrangement of the hair is most important. Bands are becoming to faces of a Grecian caste. Ringlets better suit lively and expressive heads.

Much economy of time is achieved by employing wave pieces, plaits, false switches or false frizzettes in a coiffure. These conveniences add the little details so pleasing to the eye without a lady having to sacrifice hours of toil that could be better spent elsewhere.

The practice of *enamelling* a lady's face cannot be recommended. The paste clings to the skin in such a manner that for the desired countenance to be achieved, emotions, whether they be joy or sorrow, must be suppressed. We give no credit to the malingerers who would have us believe Queen Alexandra herself enamels. There is a spiteful impulse in men and women both that cannot allow that beauty may exist without youth.

It may be stated once and for all that the practice of dyeing the hair is decidedly injurious. Ladies not blessed with the nut-brown locks so coveted today must remember that every constituent part of man tends to make the human machine one harmonious whole: the figure, the stature, the skin, the hair, the gait, &c. If the hair is dyed, what relation can exist between this new colour and the skin and eyes &c.?

The Royal disapproval of cosmetics, hair-dyes and other forms of insincerity in personal appearance is not veiled in any way. A little open comment from those in high places has worked wonders in reducing the evil.

DEBUTANTES

A debutante on the eve of being presented to the monarch often brims with little worries about the train of her dress and the twist of her hair and falls into peril of neglecting the art of her curtsey. Do not imagine that the curtsey she makes in a minuet or gavotte will suffice. A Court curtsey is much lower and requires infinite grace in its deportment.

A Court curtsey is always on the right foot on the *descent* and the left on the *ascent*. This allows the debutante to rise with a slightly backward movement, and suggests the debutante is reluctant to unnecessarily intrude.

Pay heed to the tale of the unfortunate debutante whose shoe caught in her skirts, and who was unable to rise. Although the Royal Circle kept remarkable countenance so to spare her blushes, a broad smile appeared on the King's own face as she was carried from the room after the fashion of the old childhood game 'Honey pots'.

The Queen is a lover of beauty, both in form and face. The debutante whose appearance evokes a pleased comment from Her Majesty is always safe to be one of the beauties of her first season.

SOCIAL ETIQUETTE

Out and About

On entering a restaurant and sitting down; *take off your hat*. It is only a proper mark of respect to your own class, towards whom you should *pay* the same deference you *exact* from others. We have seen men and women alike turned away from restaurants for refusing to do the courtesy.

Do not *strain* after great people – for, although they like the homage inasmuch as it flatters their vanity, yet they despise the dispenser of it. Pay them, however, all proper respect; but do not forget what is due to yourself.

Should you, whilst walking with your friend, meet an acquaintance, never introduce them. Young men in particular may think nothing of introducing a young lady of lower class to their mother or sister, little realising what mortification may be induced by forced acquaintanceship with a milliner's assistant.

Ladies who smile behind their hands at gentlemen who don their silk hats and frock coats at the seaside must beware that their own attire does not betray a similar solecism. They themselves are guilty of trimming their heavy silk and satin with glittering beads when a more suitable travel costume would consist of piques or flowered or white muslins, white shoes and white stockings. Should the weather be inclement the lady has the choice of tweed, serge and all wool-materials. The travelling costume should be of the class of tailor-mades, irregardless of the climate.

In the hands of the careless, the morning paper is a dangerous weapon, dashing fellow passengers of the omnibus in the face and all but knocking their hats off.

Our fair sisters are so peculiar regarding their rights that she often forgets chivalry has to be met with consideration on her part. We often see a lady of comfortable situation quite plump with health commandeering an inside seat in an omnibus, leaving the previous owner, a scrap of a boy, coughing piteously on the outside.

Whistling and singing are considered in poor taste on city streets, although allowed on the quiet country road. A gentleman never walks with his hands in his pockets.

Parties

There is no longer any need for a house to be turned upside down for a ball; the practice is quite disruptive and entirely out-dated. There are a great number of empty houses and pleasant hotels that may be hired and for a very economical price when one takes into consideration that all the little etceteras of décor and atmosphere will be included in the sum.

With the advent of the automobile, every inconvenience has been taken out of the picnic. It is with very great ease that we may convey the picnic hamper, another marvel of technology, often equipped with little compartments to keep butter cool, and soup hot, and whose secondary function is a table, to a carefully selected beauty spot in the countryside.

And if tea be desired in the woods, no longer is it necessary to make a fire of dry sticks and boil the water over it. Safety spirit-lamps with draught-proof stands take the place of the old primitive fashion.

When the responsibility for the picnic food is shared amongst a large party something is almost invariably forgotten; most often it is the salt, the loss of which renders many a picnic dead. Better, then, to allow the caterer to provide the fare. Many good caterers provide hot fare such as soups, or boiling water for the dyspeptic, but we find it markedly more agreeable to request cool food and eat at leisure. Cold cuts such as chicken, tongue, and beef should be accompanied by potted cheese and meat, new-baked bread, wafers and jellies, trifles and fruit tarts, and a variety of sandwiches to suit all tastes: cucumber, lobster and cress.

A masquerade offers false opportunity for indecorous behaviour for men and women alike. The mask is a flimsy disguise at best, for what an acquaintance cannot confirm by the face they can guess through mannerisms and mode of dress. It is best, then, for attendees at a masquerade to behave just as if they had no disguise at all.

Some delicacy is required in navigating today's social strata and it is to the relief of many a hostess that the garden party has passed into fashion. She may now open her garden to her estimable doctor neighbours, while the intimacy of the drawing room remains closed.

Gentlemen's Clubs

The loud-voiced man is one of the nuisances of a club. Loud talking may be endured in the smoking or general room, but certainly not in the library or the reading rooms.

A man is not a gentleman if he removes his coat or sits in his shirtsleeves in any of the public rooms. An allowance, however, is made in the billiard room.

The name of a woman should never be whispered in a club unless it is to say something complimentary of her. Even this is not in good taste.

Men are notoriously selfish in their habits in regards to newspapers at their clubs. There is no written etiquette relating to these habits although it is generally understood that the junior members will accede to the senior.

A man who dines at his club offers much relief for his wife. She no longer anxiously anticipates a telegram informing her 'Bringing home three men for dinner' but instead receives with pleasure 'Dining at club to-night'. A hastily prepared dinner is dispensed with, and instead she has the freedom to substitute a meal of her choosing accompanied by a favourite book.

Women's Clubs

It is the first instinct of society to reject that which is new, certain that they have never heard the like, yet to find that as time progresses their feelings towards the hated object softens into affection, or at the least, tolerance. So it is with women's clubs, that development of the late Victorian Era, which has done such marvels for women.

It is the simplest thing in the world for a woman to join a club. Once the lady has selected the club to which she wishes to belong she has but to send to the secretary for the requisite form. Once she has filled up the form it is really only a matter of finding a friend who is an existing member to propose her, and another to second her.

Women's clubs are not breeding grounds for women's suffrage, but rather for developing those qualities desired by a husband; compassion, unselfishness and a companionable nature.

The well-known writer Frank Danby said, 'It is as futile to argue with a bridge club maniac as with an opium eater or an inebriate'; a sentiment many will feel aptly put. An estranged relation of the genteel ladies' clubs, bridge clubs have caused mania in scores of formerly respected women. By nature, women are not moderate, and one can but wonder what portion of the housekeeping money is diverted to this unfortunate new obsession.

Sporting Pursuits

Chess clubs are all the rage. Every man who is skilled in chess will admit that the acquirement is not merely an amusing activity but an education in itself. We cannot but think that there will never be a time when chess is not enjoyed by the best of society.

The modern young man finds it convenient to be equipped with many minor accomplishments, among which he numbers: Poker, billiards, backgammon, baccarat, draughts, ecarte, vingt-et-un and loo.

There is a sad party of men who are of the impression that the only fun to be had when playing cards is from cheating. They imagine it is in their favour that they are quite honest about it, ignorant or perhaps uncaring that for their fellow players, the game is spoilt.

Cards and Calls

The etiquette for the telephone is at present no more than sensibility and common sense, and a person who behaves as though they had possession of both must rarely offend. An invitation should never be issued over the telephone for fear of engaging a person where they do not wish to be engaged, simply by dint of forward action on the behalf of the caller, and a desire not to offend on behalf of the recipient.

The card for calling and 'at homes' may range in colour only from white to ivory or cream and bear neither ornament nor border, with no discernable difference for either gender. Copperplate is the mark of true taste; it is from this the name and the address should be printed. The name should occupy the centre, with the address situated in the lower left corner, in rather smaller letter. If the owner of the card is accustomed to routine, the date should be printed on the card, if not, merely written.

A married lady leaves three cards upon departing the friend to whom she pays a visit, or upon arriving, if the friend is out. Of this number one card is her own and two her husband's. If the caller is unmarried, she should in no circumstances leave a card for the husband of the lady on whom she is calling. Likewise, if the lady called on is widowed or as yet unmarried, the caller leaves only one of her husband's cards.

It was formerly the custom to turn down the corner of a card if your visits were intended for more than one person in a family, and it is even now occasionally done; but it is much better to leave a card for each division – that is, one for the master of the house; another for the mistress; and one for the young ladies.

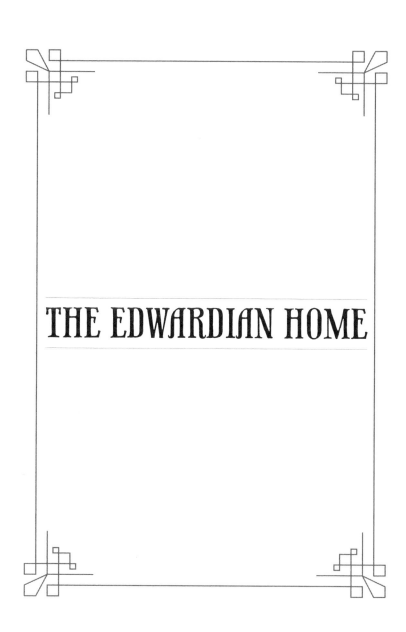

THE EDWARDIAN HOME

General Décor

While fashionable opinions may differ in regards to taste, a homemaker cannot err too greatly if she recalls the sensible words of Mrs Panton: 'Sunshine is the very first necessity of life…' To this end, heavy and unnecessary drapery is to be avoided, for this diminishes light and harbours dust, which is the enemy of comfort and hygiene.

W. Shaw Sparrow quite rightly said that 'After the fireplace, coming next in importance among the decorative essentials is the bay window.' To those critics who claim that the size of the window affords any passers-by who wish it a view of one's private goings-on, we would say a pretty sheet of lace and Florentine or Venetian blinds easily prevents this. Blinds improve the aspect of the window tenfold, and are infinitely more practical for the modern, reduced household than the drapery of yesterday.

There can be no material more hygienic than linoleum.

Mothers across the country are seeking to line their nurseries with the material, prizing it for its ease of cleaning, as well as the protection it affords the household's most precious and fragile member. We caution wives and mothers, however, to remember that linoleum is considered above the reach of many households, and indeed no wife should empty her husband's pocket merely for fashion's sake.

Those with electric light must relinquish the blue and peacock-green of their wallpaper, as the appearance is altogether too vivid, while those with gas lamps must avoid yellow, for that shade all but disappears in the light.

For a home maker conscious of her budget, and not wishing to worry at her husband's thoughts too much with her desire to 'keep up' with Mrs So-and-So, wallpaper may do very well.

Art Nouveau no longer dwells solely in Paris, its popularity in England assisted, no doubt, by the King's love of everything French.

The cosy corner improves the design of any unremarkable house. A Moor-esque fashion is suitable for cosy corners situated in smoking or billiard rooms, complementing the masculine room and its inhabitants. For the more feminine and delicate drawing room a floral or Japanese screen is the more appropriate design. We ask is there any truer comfort than being sequestered next to a fire, bookshelves within reach, and shaded from the continual demands of a busy household?

If you cannot obtain a hearth-rug that exactly corresponds with the carpet, get one entirely different; for a decided contrast looks better than a bad match.

An eminent Doctor has credited Booth's vacuum cleaner with ending the spread of Plague at an English naval barracks and we cannot think of a finer invention to combat the microbe, which so abounds in dirt and dust.

We in the modern age are fortunate that the primary concern of modern housekeeping is utility. Mrs Peel has said, 'I take it as a happy sign of the times that the "best bedroom" has been bundled out of existence along with its evil companion, the gaudy and tawdry drawing room' and indeed we could not be more in agreement. We find that a small house, with only two or three servants, offers a freedom from expense and housewifely cares.

The Kitchen

The kitchen must be decorated according to the practicalities of hygiene. Walls should imitate hospitals in their design, with rounded corners that do not attract dust. A light or white wall that may be washed is a necessity, as is a whitewashed ceiling cleaned annually.

What wife can truly dread the kitchen when she is possessed of a Mixing and Whisk machine? There are many little variations of the device to suit a lady's capriciousness and all capable of reducing egg mixture and batter to incomparable lightness with but a few revolutions of the handle.

We must draw attention to one of the many ingenious devices contriving to ease the burden of the modern labour-saving household. The *Polliwashup* is effective in eliminating the most arduous of tasks; washing up. All the device requires is a kettle of boiled water poured into its body, washing cutlery and crockery with no more effort than a turn of the handle.

The Garden

The kitchen-garden is one of the most important parts of general domestic economy, whenever the situation of a house will permit a family to avail themselves of its assistance, in aid of butchers' bills. With a little care and attention, a kitchen-garden, though small, might be rendered not only useful, but, in fact, as ornamental as a modern grass carpet. It is one objection to the adoption of a kitchen-garden in front of the dwelling, or in sight of the family apartments, that its very nature makes it an eye-sore than otherwise at all seasons. This, however, is an objection that may be readily got over by a little attention to neatness and good order.

A garden that tries its hand at every fashion can often appear to be a sad confusion of styles. There is no aesthetic pleasure in observing well trained shrubbery backing a wild tangle of baby's breath, aubretia and thyme; the two sit uncomfortably together and suggest indecision on the part of the designer.

Gertrude Jekyll avidly maintains that marble has no place in our gardens. Her claim is that stone and lead are happier materials for our gardens, originating, as they do, from our home quarries. Lead especially, with age, assumes a patina of silvery-grey that suits our garden evergreens.

The long and winding front garden path, once considered fashionable, is recognised across the land as most unfavourable for the smaller garden. What purpose can it have but to perplex the butcher's boy and make unsuspecting guests giddy?

Our King has been largely instrumental in sweeping aside old restrictions, smoking as he does almost incessantly. We advise the gardener to invite their guests to smoke in the conservatory, as they will fumigate his hot house plants with Princess Nicotine. A pretty glass bowl in the Art Deco style must be provided, as ash is not conducive to healthy soil.

HEALTH AND
WELLBEING

Late hours and anxious pursuits exhaust the nervous system, and produce disease and premature death.

To cure drunkenness, *Pears Encyclopaedia* advises us to take, 'an emetic of a tablespoonful of mustard in water, and douche the head in cold water.'

Drinking cold water when the body is hot, and hot tea and soups when cold, are productive of many evils.

We know not of anything attended with more serious consequences than that of sleeping in damp linen.

Decomposing animal and vegetable substances yield various noxious gases, which enter the lungs and corrupt the blood.

In the case of sunstroke you might do worse than loosening your dress about the neck, acting on your bowels and applying cold water to your crown.

Eat slowly and you will not over eat.

There is much more damage done by admitting visitors to invalids than is generally supposed.

For ventilation open your windows both at top and bottom. The fresh air rushes in one way, while the foul makes its exit the other. This is letting in your friend and expelling your enemy.

Keeping the feet warm will prevent headaches.

Females with slender means are for the most part destined to in-door occupations, and have but little time allotted to them for taking the air, and that little time is generally sadly encroached upon by the ceremony of dressing to go out.

Exercise in the open air is of the first importance to the human frame, yet how many are in a manner deprived of it by their own want of management of their time!

Active exercise may be enumerated walking, running, leaping, swimming, riding, fencing, the military exercise, different sorts of athletic games &c. Active exercises are more beneficial to youth, to the middle-aged, to the robust in general, and particularly to the corpulent and the plethoric.

Exercise should be begun and finished gradually, never abruptly. To continue exercise until a profuse perspiration or a great degree of weariness takes place is far from being wholesome.

It is only the rudest of wheelmen and wheelwomen that ride hastily past invalids in bath chairs or infants in their perambulators, sounding the bell suddenly and sharply.

A gentleman bicyclist, when wheeling with a lady, will give her the safer side of the road, taking care to situate himself between her and oncoming vehicles.

Tobacco smoke is reported to be preventative of malaria although there is a school of thought that proclaims chloride of lime to be its equal, if not its superior.

The health corset has done much to amend for the injuries suffered by women for Lady Fashion. Long have corsets been designed, it seems, to constrict the chest and prevent anything like a real breath of air being taken. The health corset encourages the chest forward, embracing the necessity of air without sacrificing a neat figure.

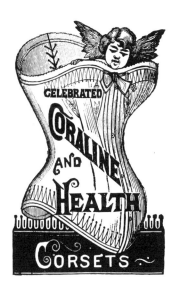

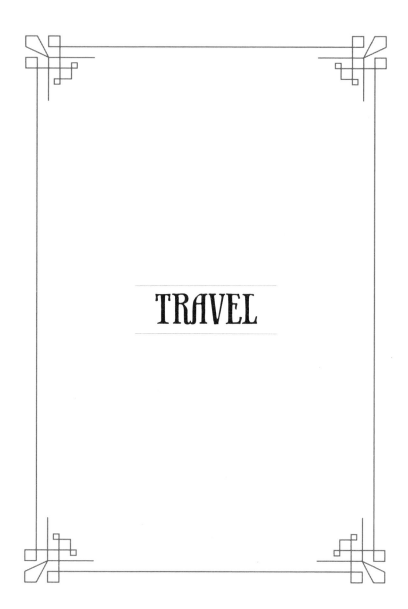

TRAVEL

An Englishman is too often convinced that English ought to be spoken all over the world, for any other tongue greatly inconveniences him. He forgets that the world will reflect back on him the sort of face he turns to it and every little endeavour on his part might come back tenfold. Those who think to display England's superiority through their cold contempt and put-on airs betray only their own bad manners and nothing of their nation's glory.

For doting parents who seek to bestow upon their daughters a true new-century education, taking her abroad for a few weeks of every spring contributes much to the formation of her mind.

The King and Queen and the Royal circle usually converse in French, and French is acknowledged as the language of polite society across Europe. Their Majesties each have two sets of visiting cards, printed in French and English, so that they may have cards in French to leave upon visits to the various Embassies and Foreign Powers. Indeed, sons and daughters of the best circles no longer regard French as an accomplishment, any more than they would regard *gloves* a *luxury*.

Travel will only improve a mind open to improvement. Travellers who find foreign churches unpleasantly situated and 'not a scratch on ours at home' and who look at Homer's landscape and find it dry and devoid of heroic scene, would be dreadful bores whether they had travelled the world or never set foot from their own doorstep.

RESOURCES

Adapted from:

Enquire Within upon Everything (1856, Houlston and Stoneman)

Hints on Etiquette, etc (1834, Messrs. Longman, Rees, Orme, Brown, Green and Longman)

Bell, Yvonne *The Edwardian Home* (2008, Osprey Publishing)

Germain, Walter *The Complete Bachelor: Manners for Men* (1896, D. Appleton and Company)

Humphry, Mrs C. E. *Manners for Women* (1897, J. Bowden)

Jennings, Anne *Edwardian Gardens* (2005, English Heritage)

Long, Helen *The Edwardian House* (1993, Manchester University Press)

Mandleberg, Hilary *Edwardian House Style: An Architectural and Interior Design Source Book* (1994, David & Charles)

TIPS FOR

HUSBANDS
& WIVES
FROM 1894

RUTH SMYTHERS

Tips For Husbands and Wives From 1894

Ruth Smythers

ISBN: 978 1 84953 195 5   Hardback   £4.99

In 1894, Ruth Smythers, 'Beloved wife of The Reverend L. D. Smythers', wrote:

'While sex is at best revolting and at worse rather painful, it has to be endured... One cardinal rule of marriage should never be forgotten: give little, give seldom and, above all, give grudgingly... Most men are by nature rather perverted, and if given half a chance, would engage in quite a variety of the most revolting practices.'

The Methodist wife didn't intend to be amusing, but this brief treatise written for young brides is side-splitting today and an eye-opener to how mores have changed in just over a century.

www.summersdale.com